LILY M. S. WHYTE

Perceptions in Verse

AUSTIN MACAULEY
PUBLISHERS LTD.

A CIP catalogue record for this title is available from the British Library.

ISBN 978-1-78612-536-1 (paperback)
ISBN 978-1-78612-537-8 (hardback)
ISBN 978-1-78612-538-5 (eBook)

www.austinmacauley.com

First Published (2016)
Austin Macauley Publishers Ltd.
25 Canada Square
Canary Wharf
London
E14 5LQ

ACKNOWLEDGEMENTS

I should like to thank the self-help group which opened my mind to the fact of a Power greater than myself. The basis of this poetry book deals with the adventure of handing my life over to this Higher Power. Following on from this I should like to acknowledge the book on enlightenment which I found really revealing.

Thanks are due to my friends Jean and Brian: writing the poems was the easy bit, the difficulty was mastering the computer, which was essential as my once good writing is now illegible. I thank them for their help and for Brian's beautiful printing of my first book of poetry.

I also dedicate this book to my family and to those who have passed away.

IN LOVING MEMORY

To a kind and gentle Mother who I loved very much and nursed her when she had a stroke. I am regretfully aware I could have been a better daughter.
RUTH STEVEN WHYTE or MITCHELL DIED 14th JUNE 1980

To my Father who was handsome and good fun at times, he was also a very stern man. My mother and father were divorced.
JAMES STIRLING WHYTE DIED FEBRUARY 20th 1985

To my husband. I lost him which was careless of me as he was inclined to stray however we stayed together as friends to his last day. He was a recovering alcoholic and when he died I received dozens of letters saying how grateful people were for his help and friendship.
JOHN BORROWMAN SINCLAIR DIED 8th NOVEMBER 1987

To my dear son Robert who was born with Spina Bifida and was paralyzed from the waist down. He married, drove a car and enjoyed life. He had a lovely sense of humour – although he could be trouble.
ROBERT GARRY SINCLAIR FORMERLY KNOWN AS KENNETH DIED 11th JULY 2010

CONTENTS

PROLOGUE

Many discoveries have come into our lives during the past eighty years. To the older generation who have known life without the benefit of technology some inventions are almost like magic. Young people happily accept the advantages while we older folk are amazed at the brilliance of the human brain.

Unfortunately there is one very important aspect to our lives which has still to be solved and that is regarding our behaviour. When you consider the pain inflicted on and suffered by individuals and populations throughout the ages we must know that something is badly wrong with us.

Since we have become expert at killing with weapons of mass destruction, clearly something has to be done. From the beginning of time we have reasoned that we have to kill the enemy before they destroy us, but before we embark on mutual annihilation could we find another way. Is it possible to love your enemies or alternatively have no enemies. We can do this by handing our lives over to a Power greater than ourselves, difficult if you do not believe in such an existence in which case we have to use our own resources. Only I for one have come to believe that nothing we have is up to the task.

The tragedy is that we have to be very badly hurt before we ask for help. When we watch our minds we are in for quite a shock. An interesting concept which I read in a book on enlightenment asks if our minds can be trusted, can we be sure they are always right, or does it depend on a personal opinion or even worse our ego. Granted our thinking is very clever and is a good tool for maths crosswords and such like. It can also be very dangerous like a torrent of water carrying us helplessly out of control. Could it be that arguments, wars, murders hatred and greed are formed in the human mind.

Until most of us come to that conclusion you will constantly have to turn the other cheek. Perhaps the best policy is to practice handing your will and life over to a Power greater than yourself. Only don't try to change others, preach at them or blame anyone. Try to be happy, negative thoughts are dangerous to your health and not really you.

FAMILY TREE

Its branches constrained
By clips of deeds long past
What freedom remains
From a ghostly path

And trailed through the seeds
In silent memory
The tree of life is twisted
From what it's meant to be

So before conception
Our lives are largely planned
By the authors of perception
Scribed by another hand

Then when we seek our freedom
To grow another way
The branch swings back to what it knows
Compelled to be that way

Yet love can disentangle
The gnarled knots of hate
Truth can point new angles
Loose ties that fascinate

Life can free the chain
From those who dominate
And God can ease our pain
And let the tree grow straight

Family Tree

THE HOUSEHOLD

It's a damaged house
A little boy was heard to say
It was cold and empty and lonely inside
And longed for a new family

Its kind strong walls like empty arms
Needed folk to hold and embrace
You came and saw its hidden charms
And made it your own dear place

You dried its damp tears
Then with paint made it bright
Healed the wounds of past years
Gave it warm fires at night

Then to change its whole aspect
And its point of view
Put in sparkling new windows
For sun and light to shine through

Now filled with pretty things
It looks really good
It has started to feel happy
Like any good home should

But by far the best for this old house
Is the warmth and fun and laughter about
Its problems are loved as much as its grace
A quiet gentle happiness in this dear old place

CIRCUMSTANCES

Surrounded by life's events
With memories having the power to last
Pillars erected to each moment
Encircling like monuments to the past

Amid this circle which bind us
Defying all efforts to explain
The circumstances that remind us
That history could repeat it all again

SPIRIT

There is a spirit of greed
That cannot be sated
There is a spirit of fear
Where anxious thoughts are created

There is a spirit of self will
Which, has a conviction of right
And can lead to ill will
Causing quarrels and fights

There is a spirit of sorrow
In a valley of tears
Hope gone for tomorrow
Sadness in future years

There is the spirit of forgiveness
When hearts and hurts are healed
In a state of quiet and stillness
The power of love revealed

There is the spirit of fun
And laughter most sweet
There is the spirit of friendship
In folk that we meet

There are the spirits of those lost
That we no longer see
There is a spirit of gratitude
For all they meant to me

There is a spirit of pride
Which predicts a fall
How do I know about these feelings
Well I have had them all

BEING A DOG

My name is Rocket
That's what they all shout
If they want me drop it or stop it
Usually I can guess what it is about

I love my people a lot
And they love me it is true
But sometimes it's just that I have got
To do what a dog has to do

When I can see what is on the table
It is more than a dog can stand
Food smells good, and if I am able
I will gobble up what ever is to hand (or paw)

The thing I hate most is thunder
The noise fills me with fear
I will hide myself in anything I can get under
And wish it would all disappear

When we are out, I am often admired
Now what else can I say
I can fall asleep when I feel tired
But sometimes I just call it a day

KINDNESS

We are given instructions
From a Higher Power from above
To turn away from destruction
And settle quarrels with love

Yet we feel we must fight
Well we are sure it is okay
Being certain of our right
So we all disobey

Then troubles continue to rage
Blood is shed again and again
Punishment given to the disgraced
And many lives are lived in pain

So try to forgive those who would do us harm
Not withstanding the effort it takes
Look kindly and use all your charm
And see if a difference it makes

QUESTIONS

Will Battles go on eternally?
Is the greater evil the winner?
Does the one who sins have to be
Hurt by another sinner?

Are there any others here
In a position to condemn?
Is to condone our greatest fear
So we have to punish them?

In a black and white idea of life
Are we ensnared by the illusion
That is a weakness to forgive?
Did a Teacher cause confusion?

Was forgiveness his real intent
And his Father's point of view?
Could it be he said what he meant?
And did he say we much do it too?

Winter

WINTER

Winter white with frosty lace
Bright orange sun's reflected face
On icy mirror and soft snow
Still and quiet yet shimmering glow

Winters seasons changing face
A different world in the same place
Now brown earth and wind and rain
And stark branch revealed again

Simplicity of winter line
Naked truth of resting time
Taking back from plant and tree
And hiding what has yet to be

Auntie's Seaside Cottage

AUNTIE'S SEASIDE COTTAGE

I often recall when the children were small
Aunt Mamie's cottage at Maidens
I think of the summers we came in great numbers
And remember how welcome you made us

I am really amazed looking back on these days
That wee house was truly fantastic
'Twas not made of stone, well, not stone alone
Sand Cottage was mostly elastic

If I can recount the total amount
Of folk who came one year to stay
It will take me some time to make it rhyme
Here goes – I'll try anyway

There were
Mamie and Ronnie and Big Brother Johnnie
Alan and Karen and Betty and Bill
There were Ronald and Janey
And if that sounds too many
Don't you believe it there were more people still

There were
Young brother Billy and in-law Lily
Steven and Kenny (now Robert in fact)
If that seems too many well don't you believe it
Why shouldn't the neighbours get into the act

There were
Katherine and Shirley and Donald and Mary
Midge and her crowd would come to the door
Friends and Relations and whole congregations
Squeezed into Sand Cottage, there's aye room for more

There was
Auntie Mamie herself that remarkable lady
Who attracted such wealth of kith and kin
Thank you dear auntie for all that you've done
And thanks for fitting us in

THE VISITOR

Uninvited she walked past
Very smartly clad in brown
The old collie dog just stared aghast
At the small figure moving around

As she went from kitchen to hall
She left her calling card for me to find
Nerves she seemed to have not at all
So I cleaned up what she left behind

Charmed by her presence
I admired her fearless poise
Every morning she was present
For a breakfast of her choice

One day there appeared a beautiful fellow
With shining black feathers looking great
His beak was of the brightest yellow
But he was very irate with his mate

His shrill cry kept sounding alarm
Come out it is not safe to remain
Those people could do you a lot of harm
So my guest never returned again.

COMPULSION

Our minds could be unreliable
And we can't assume they are true
Or you may find you are liable
To do what is not wise to do

We are sometimes held by a compulsion
To behave in many strange ways
Even though there may be revulsion
The desire to act still stays

So whenever problems arise
And grip you or another
You can use your best efforts to survive
But still need God's help to recover

HEAVEN

Can we begin to understand
The promise of a heaven
How can we build a better land
Without any help or instruction

If we do it on our own
Could evil be destroyed
But as manifestly shown
The world just gets annoyed

If heaven is a personal state
Perhaps a better being would evolve
With effort and help we could create
A Kingdom where trouble is solved

THE PRANK

They were all sitting down to dine
Each at their own place
With eyes closed and an attitude sublime
While father said the grace

Isa, a tomboy, always getting a row
Planned a shock revelation
So when every head was bent in a bow
She decided to cause a sensation

The beetroot jar looked blood red
And thinking it to be a great joke
With the back of a knife and pretending she bled
Quickly drew it across her throat

In horror the family stared at Isa
Red juice running down her neck for all to see
Her mother who was sitting beside her
Soon put a stop to her daughter's glee

THE THOUGHT PROCESS

Be the watcher of your mind
See if it follows your emotion
Watch if you follow as if blind
Question your motivation

Could it be envy planting a cruel seed
Ambition is good if you are not driven
Disregard any feelings of greed
Hurtful thoughts may come unbidden

If only you could make it stop
Like turning off a radio
Minds tormented by constant talk
Value silence – let it go

FINDHORN

Blue seas and soft white sand
A perfect spot for a holiday
Findhorn a place of great charm
A haven for the children and me

Our caravan's panoramic view
Of sand dunes on the shore
The gentle sound of lapping waves
You could not ask for more

I placed baby on a rug
Outside the kitchen door
I watched as he contented lay
While I sat on the floor

Then almost without warning
The window was curtained black
Thousands of bees were swarming
I feared we were under attack

With baby outside, I got such a fright
But his chubby arms were waving
And he was gurgling with delight
It seemed he didn't want saving

I thought the bees said don't be alarmed
He will come to no harm
Then I closed the door shut tight
With gratitude that we were alright

THE PRAYER

I try to remember each day
On being hurt or unjustly accused
I may have hurt another in some way
With apologies accepted or refused

The prayer so often repeated
To allow God's will to be done
How can we say we've succeeded
When in truth we hope we have won

Our wish is to be excused and saved
Forgiven to the extent we forgive
Trespasses and debts may be waived
With happiness given as long as we live

TIME

Time flows like a river or a stream
Carrying memories of events long gone
Floating past as in a dream
Recalled to mind by a poem or song

The child has grown into a man
By some abstract force of change
Time which has a visible plan
That cause us to grow and age

Pure and clean the water of life
That's present in every soul
If undefiled by fear and strife
May enable us to live ever more

Water filtered to a clean state
And cleaned of all pollutions
Free of all that could contaminate
And rid our minds of all illusions

THE WEDDING OF CLARE AND STEVE

Congratulations Mr and Mrs Blakemore
Now you have tied the knot
An abundance of joy for you is in store
Because you deserve a lot

Love comes to those who wait
That is true for Steve and Clare
Today they entered the marital state
With friends and family invited to share

Their family is charming and polite
A credit to both parents
Clare and Steve have every right
To feel proud of their achievements

Clare has great ability to amaze
Because nothing is too much trouble
Her kindness leaves me in a daze
Our laughter often bends me double

A couple who find time easy to share
And are helpful to everyone
Are they aware, how much we care
Bless you both and have lots of fun

AN EXPERIENCE

I was in Glasgow; it was a cold foggy day in 1950. I was walking in the more elite district where there are large houses in red sandstone. I was making my way to a new friend's home and this was my first visit. I was invited to afternoon tea by the daughter of the house, whom I had befriended recently at our mutual place of employment and as I went through the smog, conscious of the dirt and smoke which made your face and clothes black, I wished I looked more respectable.

At last I came upon my destination, and rang a very haughty sounding bell. A loud deep bark resounded through the house, followed by a kind welcome from an attractive lady. I gratefully entered and was pleased to see a large fire burning brightly in the lounge. When introductions and greetings were completed a trolley of goodies was brought forth, consisting of Scottish bridies and more elegant sandwiches, followed by delicious squashy cream cake.

I found my new friends to be charming and entertaining. The good company and warmth of the environment made the following time most pleasant. Eventually I rose and announced my forthcoming departure. Conscious that my journey home may take some time, I asked to be directed to the bathroom and was sent up a large curved stair which at its summit was the biggest bathroom I've ever seen. I climbed the stairs and because it was a long way from the lounge and I didn't anticipate taking long I left the bathroom door ajar. That was my mistake. The Alsatian, who had been polite and gentle in the lounge entered the bathroom and fixed stern eyes on my person as I was in an undignified situation. I spoke to him gently and the response was aloud growl. Undeterred I tried to stand up He dared me and the effect was frightening I considered my options, I could call for help but owing to the delicacy of my situation I refrained from doing so. Time passed with no move from either party. After what seemed like an eternity the dog was summoned by his mistress and departed I was very relieved and followed him downstairs keeping a safe distance.

Finally I said thank you and my appreciation for a lovely afternoon. The dog and I looked at each other and we agreed to keep our secret. This I have done for fifty years but at last I have told the embarrassing story of the Alsatian who held me prisoner in the bathroom.

MEMORIES

The March wind playfully whipped at the young woman as she bent over the steps she was cleaning. As she worked transferring, the white of the cleaning stone to the step, her thoughts strayed to the events leading to her present condition. The boy she loved was not her husband or the father of her child. He belonged to her past, the happier carefree days. She dreamed of the laughter and love with a sense of longing. In her memory her mother's voice came to mind – *you don't want to marry him*. It was the age old advice, well meant but mistaken – of one generation to another.

Ruth was a pretty and compliant young girl, anxious to please her mother, so it was she married Jim.

Jim was very handsome and charming he was also a Peter Pan who had no idea what it meant to be a husband and a father. He was the product of a stern overbearing man, a master grocer used to being obeyed by his staff, and his beautiful young wife who adored her son Jim. So it was when Father spoke to Jim, calling him "my Boy" not in an affectionate manner, as it nearly always was preceded by a gruff demand to his son to smarten up his ideas an order no doubt needed, but also deeply resented. Jim gravitated to his gentle loving mother who comforted and spoilt him. Thus began a lifelong habit of using women, yet he never respected them. Respect, he felt, was for domineering people – like his father.

Ruth struggled with her situation for some time, then one day things came to a head. "Where are you going ?" she asked as she watched her husband getting dressed;

she already knew the answer for he was already wearing jodhpurs.

"Going to take Yarrow out for a bit." Yarrow was Jim's pride and joy, a beautiful sleek white horse.

"There is no milk for the baby; give me some money, I shall have to get some food anyway."

"Okay," Jim replied, "I will get money for you on my way home."

Ruth looked at him in disbelief; she had heard this before and waited in vain.

"Won't be long," he said, shutting the door behind him as he spoke. Then as if on cue her four month old wailed in protest. Ruth fed her daughter with what she could find in the empty cupboard, then packed her bags and went home to her mother.

It was to be over twelve years before Ruth and her child met Jim again.

This story began in the 1930s; they settled into a sedate and gentle life with her grandmother. They lived in a small neat bungalow furnished with rather heavy old fashioned table, chairs and sideboard which had been downsized from the large family home, inhabited by the Mitchell family before bereavement and marriage diminished the need for a large house.

ABOUT BABIES

When was the baby boom? I can't remember the year, but I know for sure that in 1962 there was a baby boom in our road in Inverness. I had to go to Raigmore Hospital for my pre-natal check up, so I set out in my first car which was a small A30; I was really quite proud of it. On arriving at the hospital, I was rather surprised to see other mums-to-be: while some were just familiar faces, others I knew as friends. We got talking of course and I invited to give them a lift home. One lady was having twins I remember. An important part of this story is that the hospital was on a very steep hill: you may have guessed what happened. The heavily pregnant ladies heaved themselves into the small car and we set off home. I really tried to get up the hill, but the car laden with nine bodies (that's including babies) just couldn't manage. So I had to tell them to get out and walk up the hill where I waited for them. They struggled and squeezed themselves back into the car. Eventually we arrived home, and as I remember it nobody laughed. Later on when I recalled the story we thought it hilarious.

CAR TROUBLE

It had been a unusually mild winter in Inverness, but on the day we moved to Dumfries it snowed. There was no sign that morning of just what the weather had in store as we embarked on our journey.

John, my husband, waited for the removal men to finish packing while I set off in my rather dilapidated Hillman Husky with our two boys. I fixed up the back of the car with a rug for them to sit on and some toys hopefully to keep them amused on the long journey. You must remember that in those days there were no such things as safety seats for children. In fact I cannot recall anything about having to have an MOT certificate, which it may have passed as fortunately the car had a strong engine. Before setting off I had given Steven my eldest a tablet because he got car sick. The other little boy who was born disabled and I'd left his wheelchair for the removal van, thinking to leave more room in the car. I was advised to travel through a place called the Small Glen thus avoiding the busy main roads. Before we had gone very far the snow came down thick and fast until there was a complete white out. It was difficult to see, but there was actually very little to see except a few cars abandoned in ditches here and there, and the outline of a solitary house on a distant hill. As the snow got deeper I put the car into first gear, and we limped slowly along. By this time I knew we were in trouble, if the car stalled I doubted my ability to carry both the boys in the snow, and we were miles from anywhere with not a soul in sight. Eventually, alternating through panic and prayer, we reached Perth, and I thankfully found a garage who was willing to sell me another old car. Leaving my burnt out Hillman with a tearful thank you for its mammoth effort we continued our journey, after a rest, to my friend in Paisley. The following day we travelled to Dumfries and our new house. Looking back on our adventure I thought it was lucky the old car had the breakdown and not me.

FREEDOM OF MIND

Prison could be a place where freedom is found
Some things are not as they seem to be
Silence is heard when truth is spoken aloud
Thoughts and lessons with a different reality

Serenity and peace can be taught
Although difficult problems abound
Minds that are tormented and fraught
Can learn to be still quiet and sound

ABOUT FLOWERS

The dandelion rests his yellow head
Sleeping rough in the street
While flowers more gently bred
Have beds well tended and neat

Bluebells like an army
Marching among woods and trees
Their uniforms neat and charming
A picture as blue as the seas

A host of golden daffodils
Trumpet sounds of glory
Proclaiming their presence in the hills
Telling a well known story

The little snowdrop white and pure
Facing the wintry blast
Delicate yet able to endure
Till the cold snow is past

A soft carpet of grass or lawn
Food for cattle or sheep
Pleasant for people to walk on
Or lie in the sun and sleep

Let us look and wonder
At all there is to admire
All the beauty around us
Given by God to inspire

Bluebells

Stillness

STILLNESS

When thoughts are stilled
Allowing space for knowing
Life is quiet and fulfilled
With love overflowing

When silence is heard in peace
You come to the conclusion
You can overcome grief
Pain may be an illusion

It's not that you are above
The usual human plight
Just dilute it with forgiving love
Let go and let God make it right

If you find it hard to take
And are afraid that you may falter
On finding you have made a mistake
Then it is your choice to alter

THE BEST

The greatest human urge
Is to be the first
The self always wants to be the best
And has to prove it to the rest

Another goal to which we could inspire
Is to try to eliminate all desire
Neither wanting to be or not to be
But allow things to be just as they are

It could be a liberation
To live with out anticipation
Granted this a different point of view
I also know it may not suit you

DELICATE BLUE

Blended to a delicate blue
The sky laced with white
Streaked across with a purple hue
Engulfed by diminishing light

Silently our minds grow still
Touching our souls with quiet refrain
Leaving our hearts to the approaching night
Freeing our thoughts from every strain

Morning brings sun and new power
Colour paints everything fresh and new
Bees search for nectar in every flower
Birds and insects bathe in the sweet dew

COMPUTER

Although I am a grown up
Well alas really I am quite old
Sometimes I find myself badly stuck
And have to wait to be told

The computer has me bamboozled
With a very strange vocabulary
Words that are unusual
Do not mean the same to me

Still I have learned to Log on
And mastered shopping on line
I can now buy from Amazon
It can really save some time

A new way of communicating
To one who is eighty four years young
What an embarrassing state of affairs
To learn from a great grandson

HOME

Once this was a home for five
But since many years have past
Now I am the only one to occupy
I can assume I will be the last

Things are gently falling
Like leaves from a tree
And parts of my life are failing
Becoming just a memory

Loss of friends is hard to bare
Making you feel very forlorn
Missing the laughter and fun you used to share
Leaving you quite alone

THE HUMAN MIND

What thoughts are you producing
Why do circumstances rule the mind
Why is our behaviour linked to what is happening
Why can we not detach when life is unkind

What would be the result if we could achieve this
Using will power seldom is a success
If only a miracle could come to relieve us
Then our world would be in less of a mess

TROUBLED THOUGHTS

A concept may cause you pain
Followed by a controlling emotion
Just watch your thinking and refrain
From feelings that harbour destruction

Circumstances which affect the mind
Stifling the joy of life and peace
On observing your thinking you may find
That letting go is a way of release

Jello

JELLO

The cutest little dog
You ever saw
Comes running to see
His favourite show

Watching with avid interest
That would make you smile
The programme that fascinates him
Is – *Country File*

It is the animals that excite him
The pigs sheep and cows
That delight him
With tail wagging joy

Cartoon characters too
Holds his attention
I must just mention
Animals that are in the zoo

A lovely little fellow
With long ears and big brown eyes
Known by the name of Jello
A spaniel called King Charles

ABOUT THE CROMARTY FIRTH

Soft green hills descending
Tumbling into the deep blue sea
The colours gently blending
To a painting of natural beauty

Nestling between the trees
Halfway down the hillside
A cottage whose paraffin lamps revealed
Softly lit windows glowing inside

The wood fire burning in the old range
Gleaming through the dusky sky
Thinking things would never change
But it was a way of life saying good bye

CHILDREN IN A WAR

Children in pain
Wounded and bereaved
Calling for a parent
For comfort and relief

Children in a war zone
Don't care who is victorious
All they want is to go home
And the fighting to be over

Pictures of the young
In a terrible situation
Those who caused such pain
Some day will say never never again

CHILDREN AT HOME

Arguments in the home
Can leave deep sorrow and wounds
Children with loyalties torn
Can become rebellious and rude

A well known poet once wrote
I quote the famous line
The child is the father of the man
A fact proven many a time

While babies born with different traits
Characters may run though a family tree
Love can mellow a lot of past mistakes
Softening the pull of ancestry

THE STORM

Sailing on the ocean
A storm came without warning
Causing panic and commotion
Among those in fear of drowning

The Master bid the storm –be still
And wind and waves did his will
A miracle is that they did obey
The story is told to this very day

Our life is like the boat we sail
The storm is our emotion
Our panic is in thinking we may fail
Our distress is the fear of coping

Our Saviour is the Higher Power
Who bids our will subside
Our helper is the one who stays
Forever by our side

WORDS THAT HIDE

I wonder where my words hide
Even those that I know very well
Are they still somewhere inside
Lying behind some dormant cell

It is strange that in conversation
I mislay the correct words I need
Friends try to help with a suggestion
But seldom do they seem to succeed

Then when I finally admit defeat
Or just as I about to go to sleep
Now when it is too late – I remember
Well I suppose it will just have to keep

AN AIR RAID

When the sirens suddenly wailed
A warning of an air raid
It would be unusual if you failed
To find a place of safety

So everyone in our home
Hurried to the Anderson shelter
Every one except my grandmother
Although we all tried hard to help her

Imagine the consternation
When grandma refused to relent
But fortunately after some persuasion
She agreed and under the bed – she went

I remember the feeling of dismay
Watching the undignified manoeuvre
I never dreamed I would see the day
I would witness such outlandish behaviour

In spite of any real danger
No one was hurt that's a fact
Though my gran was under pressure
Her pride was left intact

WORLD WAR ONE

A family of seven pictured in a pose
Taken before the onset of world war one
As yet unaware of the hell that arose
With cruel and dreadful deeds done

In the photograph were two young men
My uncles not long out of their teens
I hope unaware of what was to befall them
The end of all their hopes and dreams

As I look at the hundred year old picture in sepia
Thinking of the young boys who perished
As for my grandmother – I grieve for her
And for the children that she cherished

My family

LESSONS

How has it transpired
I think I can hazard a guess
Poems usually have been inspired
From situations in the past

Lessons that have been hard to learn
But as life's finals are getting near
I think I understand a bit at last
Some things are becoming clear

What is still more confusing and
may prevent you from getting in a state
Is to go through the process of refusing
To allow your thinking to dominate

Your thoughts may not be what you require
May not be what you need
The ability to forgive is all you have to desire
And prayer for the power to succeed

TALES FROM THE PAST

Stories I thought lost in the past
Dredged up from a recess in my brain
I had thought them too inconsequential to last
But somehow they seem to remain

Other stories I choose not to remember
It is not that I cannot recall
It's because of the heartache and trauma
I don't wish to recount it all

Your real life is true and very valuable
Sometimes difficult circumstances arise
They may feel cruel and insolvable
But ultimately LIFE and LOVE is the prize

THE MILKMAN

When I was a child of three
The lamplighter came every night
And what seemed miraculous to me
I watched as he made small pools of light

Soon there came the demise of gas
Electric light was here to stay
The lamplighter's job relegated to the past
And the night made as bright as the day

Another change came during my young years
It now seems unimportant of course
But at the time I was reduced to tears
When Willie the milkman got rid of his horse

Milk kept on the back of his cart
Was held in a very large urn
Filling the jug from a lovely brass tap
But sadly Willie left never to return

THE STUDENT

In the early days of nineteen fifty
A young girl began a new career
Although questioning her ability
She was convinced there was nothing to fear

The responsibility for caring
For others in need
The thought was slightly scary
She hoped that she would succeed

When on night shift
And was made to go where required
Then when a poor old soul passed on
Or to put it bluntly – died

The senior nurse left the girl on her own
The old man fell on his back
The air in his body caused a loud groan
Our student nurse felt under attack

Nerves made her laugh out loud
Which in a sleeping ward – not a good idea
The senior nurse came back and gave her a good slap
And that's how you deal with hysteria

THE ARGUMENT

When people are unfair
Then I tell them as gently as I am able
When those people are still unaware
Then I put my cards on the table

I shall do my best to refrain
From anger or a fight
But if it turns out to be in vain
And I can not put it right

Then I have to make the choice
Of whether or not I should let it be
If I am willing not to raise my voice
Then I have the right answer for me

MIND CHATTER

I wish that I could stop at will
The chatter in my head
But when I try to make it still
I think of many things instead

I wonder what I should have to eat
Then remember things long past
I contemplate about people that I meet
And consider how long things will last

When I have to make a decision
I find my mind keeps changing
I cannot choose which one to use
It is really quite amazing

My mind is very volatile
I hope it will be still some day
And I can train it to be quiet a while
When I try to compose what to say

Having or Being

HAVING OR BEING

Can you perceive,
A state of having or being
Or do you believe
What the world is seeing?

We are what we have
That is a common view
But all that you own
Never is truly you

Wanting power and control
As in tyrant or boss
as you reach your goal
Your real self may be lost

Those who led by example
Like teachers of the past
Found all they had was ample
And craving was gone at last

CONSCIENCE

Are we conscious
Conscious of what?
Of self and selfish thoughts
Guaranteed to confuse us

If we are not led up the garden path
By a false self made mind
We find a better place at last
A world where we are kind

Suffering can be relieved
By letting go of our will
To a Higher Power revealed
On learning to be quiet and still

Anything may be called truth
But a name does not make it proven
It may be a mirror of your mind
Or something else you have chosen

Our life is joy and even more
Home of our real self and belief
While love makes our true energy flow
Forgiveness dissolves guilt and grief

THE POET'S DILEMMA

Can you spare a moment before you go
There is something I should love to know
While I would prefer you were not too rude
Please tell me if these poems are any good

I am not hoping for a compliment
Though I would accept what is truly meant
If the verdict is not pleasing – then I suppose
The only thing to do is to recompose

I can write of anything that comes to mind
Things that are pleasant others a bit unkind
Still I have to accept whatever you say
And I suppose I can try again some other day

ABOUT THE AUTHOR

Lily Whyte was born in a district in Glasgow in 1931 and educated initially at Paisley Grammar School. When her family moved to Troon in Ayrshire she continued her education at Marr College. After her marriage in 1960 she moved to Inverness where her two sons were born. Their next home was in Dumfries; then finally, because of her husband's work, they settled in Stratford-upon-Avon in Warwickshire.

The author with Jello